P9-ARZ-644

Examining Issues Through POLITICAL CARTOONS

Iraq

Examining Issues Through POLITICAL CARTOONS

Iraq

Titles in the Examining Issues Through Political Cartoons series include:

EXAMINING ISSUES THROUGH
POLITICAL CARTOONS

Iraq

Edited by Laura K. Egendorf

Daniel Leone, *President*
Bonnie Szumski, *Publisher*
Scott Barbour, *Managing Editor*

GREENHAVEN
PRESS®

THOMSON
————★————™
GALE

San Diego • Detroit • New York • San Francisco • Cleveland
New Haven, Conn. • Waterville, Maine • London • Munich

LIBRARY OF CONGRESS CATALOGING-IN-PUBLICATION DATA

Iraq / Laura K. Egendorf, book editor.
    p. cm. — (Examining issues through political cartoons)
Includes bibliographical references and index.
ISBN 0-7377-2288-6 (lib. alk. paper) — ISBN 0-7377-2289-4 (pbk. : alk. paper)
    1. Iraq War, 2003—Caricatures and cartoons. 2. United States—Politics and
government—2001—Caricatures and cartoons. I. Egendorf, Laura K., 1973–   .
II. Series.

DS79.76.I725 2004
956.7044'3—dc21

                                                                2003047287

Printed in the United States of America

20.95

Contents

Foreword

Political cartoons, also called editorial cartoons, are drawings that do what editorials do with words—express an opinion about a newsworthy event or person. They typically appear in the opinion pages of newspapers, sometimes in support of that day's written editorial, but more often making their own comment on the day's events. Political cartoons first gained widespread popularity in Great Britain and the United States in the 1800s when engravings and other drawings skewering political figures were fashionable in illustrated newspapers and comic magazines. By the beginning of the 1900s, editorial cartoons were an established feature of daily newspapers. Today, they can be found throughout the globe in newspapers, magazines, and online publications and the Internet.

Art Wood, both a cartoonist and a collector of cartoons, writes in his book *Great Cartoonists and Their Art*:

> Day in and day out the cartoonist mirrors history; he reduces complex facts into understandable and artistic terminology. He is a political commentator and at the same time an artist.

The distillation of ideas into images is what makes political cartoons a valuable resource for studying social and historical topics. Editorial cartoons have a point to express. Analyzing them involves determining both what the cartoon's point is and how it was made.

Sometimes, the point made by the cartoon may be one that the reader disagrees with, or considers offensive. Such cartoons expose readers to new ideas and thereby challenge them to analyze and question their own opinions and assumptions. In some extreme cases, cartoons provide vivid examples of the thoughts that lie behind heinous acts; for example, the cartoons created by the Nazis illustrate the anti-Semitism that led to the mass persecution of Jews.

Examining controversial ideas is but one way the study of political cartoons can enhance and develop critical thinking skills. Another aspect to cartoons is that they can use symbols to make their point quickly. For example, in a cartoon in *Euthanasia*, Chuck Asay depicts supporters of a legal "right to die" by assisted suicide as vultures. Vultures are birds that eat dead and dying animals and are often a symbol of repulsive and cowardly predators who take advantage of those who have met misfortune or are vulnerable. The reader can infer that Asay is expressing his opposition to physician-assisted suicide by suggesting that its supporters are just as loathsome as vultures. Asay thus makes his point through a quick symbolic association.

An important part of critical thinking is examining ideas and arguments in their historical context. Political cartoonists (reasonably) assume that the typical reader of a newspaper's editorial page already has a basic knowledge of current issues and newsworthy people. Understanding and appreciating political cartoons often requires such knowledge, as well as a familiarity with common icons and symbolic figures (such as Uncle Sam's representing the United States). The need for contextual information becomes especially apparent in historical cartoons. For example, although most people know who Adolf Hitler is, a lack of familiarity with other German political figures of the 1930s may create difficulty in fully understanding cartoons about Nazi Germany made in that era.

Providing such contextual information is one important way that Greenhaven's Examining Issues Through Political Cartoons series seeks to make this unique and revealing resource conveniently accessible to students. Each volume presents a representative and diverse collection of political cartoons focusing on a particular current or historical topic. An introductory essay provides a general overview of the subject matter. Each cartoon is then presented with accompanying information including facts about the cartoonist and information and commentary on the cartoon itself. Finally, each volume contains additional informational resources, including listings of books, articles, and websites; an index; and (for historical topics) a chronology of events. Taken together, the contents of each anthology constitute an amusing and informative resource for students of historical and social topics.

Introduction

On April 9, 2003, all eyes were on Baghdad's Shahid Square. It was in that plaza that a horde of Iraqi citizens, with assistance from American soldiers, knocked over a giant statue of their leader, Saddam Hussein. The symbolic overthrow of Saddam Hussein paralleled the entrance of coalition troops (primarily American and British soldiers, with additional troops provided by Australia and Poland) into Baghdad; while the troops fired their weapons at the Iraqi army, joyful citizens threw stones at the statue. After twenty-four years of tyranny, Saddam had been deposed. The end of major fighting in Iraq followed several weeks later.

President George W. Bush's campaign to topple Saddam Hussein's regime through military means illustrates the change in America's approach to foreign policy following the September 11, 2001, terrorist attacks on the World Trade Center and the Pentagon. Those attacks made it clear that American soil was not immune from direct assault by international terrorist groups. In response, the Bush administration abandoned its noninterventionist stance and adopted a "doctrine of preemption": the idea that the United States must pursue countries with ties to terrorism, or which possess the materials needed to build weapons of mass destruction, before they attack America. This policy approach has come to be known as the "Bush Doctrine."

The "Axis of Evil"

Four and a half months after the September 11 attacks, President Bush detailed his foreign policy goals in his 2002 State of the Union address. In the speech, he targeted three nations that he considered as posing a terrorist threat—Iraq, Iran, and North Korea—and labeled them the "Axis of Evil." Focusing specifically on Iraq, Bush said,

> The Iraqi regime has plotted to develop anthrax, and nerve gas, and nuclear weapons for over a decade. This is a regime that has already used poison gas to murder thousands of its own citizens—leaving the bodies of mothers huddled over their dead children. This is a regime that agreed to international inspections—then kicked out the inspectors. This is a regime that has something to hide from the civilized world. States like these, and their terrorist allies, constitute an axis of evil, arming to threaten the peace of the world. By seeking weapons of mass destruction, these regimes pose a grave and growing danger.[1]

In June 2002, at a commencement address at West Point, Bush elaborated on his administration's new approach to foreign policy. In that speech, he outlined the Bush Doctrine and declared,

> Containment is not possible when unbalanced dictators with weapons of mass destruction can deliver those weapons on missiles or secretly provide them to terrorist allies. . . . If we wait for threats to fully materialize, we will have waited too long.
>
> We must take this battle to the enemy, disrupt his plans and confront the worst threats before they emerge.[2]

The Bush Doctrine altered more than two centuries of U.S. foreign policy. From George Washington onward, the United States typically did not go to war unless it was attacked or there was a clear indication of imminent threats, such as visual proof that enemy troops were mobilizing. In his farewell address, George Washington had urged the United States to limit its political involvement with other nations, and most of his successors followed his isolationist path, avoiding American involvement in international conflicts unless there was no other choice. For example, the United States was staunchly neutral when the Great War (later known as World War I) began in 1914. The government wavered in its decision to remain neutral after the 1915 sinking of the British passenger liner *Lusitania* by a German submarine. However, the United States did not break off relations with Germany until February

1917, following Germany's declaration that it would rely on submarine warfare to defeat the powerful British navy, and did not enter the Great War until April 6, 1917. A generation later, the United States provided arms to the British military with the Lend-Lease Act, but American troops did not enter World War II until the Japanese attack on Pearl Harbor. In other cases, such as the Korean War, the United States not only did not instigate the war but entered only as part of a United Nations coalition. Regardless of its reasons for entering a conflict, the American government usually shied away from the role of aggressor.

In some cases the United States has gone to war in response to attacks that may not have happened. The entrance into the Spanish-American War was prompted by widespread belief in America that Spain was responsible for the sinking of the battleship USS *Maine*, even though the Spanish military could not be linked to the tragedy. Congress granted President Lyndon B. Johnson war-making powers after it was informed that North Vietnamese boats had fired on U.S. ships in the Gulf of Tonkin. Congress's decision resulted in the commencement of bombing and troop deployments that would continue for more than a decade. Later investigations suggest that the Gulf of Tonkin assault may have been a fabrication. In both of these cases, it is unclear whether the nation's leaders were responding to genuinely perceived threats or had simply fabricated the news of the attacks in order to justify military action. In either case, the policy of military nonintervention was followed; the leaders did not engage in war until attacked, or at least purportedly attacked.

Opponents of the Bush Doctrine assert that reliance on military force could create an image of the United States as the world's bully; a nation that ignores internationally recognized rules of war. In an article for the *American Prospect*, George Soros, the founder of the Open Society Institute, wrote, "A dominant faction within the Bush administration believes that international relations are relations of power. Because we are unquestionably the most powerful, they claim, we have earned the right to impose our will on the rest of the world."[3] Such uses of military prowess, critics maintained, could not only fuel hatred of the United States in the Arab world but also alienate American allies. Other people, such as former secretary of state Henry Kissinger, have opined that the Bush

Doctrine may violate international laws, which sanction use of force only in response to actual threats.

Despite these concerns, the White House did not turn away from its plans to go to war against nations that supported terrorist activities, even if those countries had yet to pose an imminent threat to the United States. In fact, the Bush Doctrine had been implemented, though not under that name, soon after September 11. The Taliban, the fundamentalist Muslim regime that had controlled Afghanistan since the mid-1990s, was known to provide financial support to Osama bin Laden and the al-Qaeda terrorist network, the people behind the September 11 attacks. In October 2001 the United States demanded that Taliban leader Mullah Omar turn over bin Laden and other al-Qaeda figures. When Omar refused, U.S. forces bombed Afghanistan for two months. This war was an example of the doctrine of preemption because although the Taliban did not directly attack the United States, its support of al-Qaeda helped make possible the September 11 tragedy and, the White House feared, future attacks. The war ended with the collapse of the Taliban, but bin Laden could not be found despite extensive searching throughout Afghanistan. As of July 2003, bin Laden had not been located, although the United States has captured and killed many al-Qaeda leaders.

Saddam Hussein's Emergence

Once the battle in Afghanistan had ended, the White House turned its attention toward Iraq. The focus on Iraq, and especially on Saddam Hussein, is not surprising. For more than a dozen years, Saddam was seen by the U.S. government as one of the world's most dangerous leaders. The earliest years of his rule, which began in 1979, proved he had few qualms about using violence against fellow Iraqis, including the non-Arab Kurdish minority.

However, it was not until Saddam sought to expand Iraq's territory by invading neighboring Kuwait in August 1990 that the international community became fully aware of his thirst for power, particularly his desire to gain control of Kuwait's oil fields. Western industrialized nations feared that Saddam's landgrab would interrupt the flow of oil. Saudi Arabia's fields were also in danger because Saddam moved troops to the border Iraq shared with that nation.

Iraq's actions garnered very little international support. A thirty-nine-nation coalition, including the United States, Britain, France, and Saudi Arabia, pressured Iraq to leave Kuwait. The United Nations enacted trade sanctions that prevented Iraq from exporting oil or importing goods from other nations in hopes that Iraq's economy would collapse and Saddam would be forced to withdraw from Kuwait. The tactic failed; Iraq refused to leave the territory of its southern neighbor, and on January 16, 1991, Operation Desert Storm—a coalition effort headed by the United States—began. International forces bombed Iraq, waiting until February to enter Kuwait. Four days after troops stepped on Kuwaiti soil, Iraq agreed to a cease-fire; the war had lasted forty-three days. However, although Iraq did withdraw from Kuwait, Saddam Hussein remained in power. While the toppling of Saddam's regime would possibly have improved the quality of life for Iraqis and their neighbors, that was not the goal of the UN forces. The coalition was more focused on protecting Kuwait's sovereignty.

It was after the war's conclusion that the United States (led by George W. Bush's father, President George H.W. Bush), the UN, and other key nations and organizations grew increasingly concerned about Saddam Hussein's ability to launch deadly attacks against his rivals in the Middle East and throughout the world. Saddam was ordered by the UN Security Council in April 1991 to destroy his nation's long-range ballistic missiles and abolish Iraq's biological, chemical, and nuclear weapons programs. Saddam had already shown his willingness to use chemical weapons; mustard gas and chemical agents had been utilized against the Kurds, an ethnic minority centered in northern Iraq. For the next seven and a half years, the UN tried to send weapons inspectors to Iraq to determine the true breadth of the country's weapons programs, but Saddam's government continually obstructed the search teams. For example, in 1993 the UN Special Commission (UNSCOM, which the United Nations established to handle the nonnuclear weapons inspections) was barred from flying into Iraq.

Reports issued in early 1999 by UNSCOM and the International Atomic Energy Agency (IAEA), which conducted the nuclear weapons search, indicated that Iraq had hidden some evidence of its weapons programs. While the inspectors supervised the destruction of hundreds of ballistic missiles and nearly seven hundred tons of chemical agents, the agencies acknowledged that they could not prove that all weapons of mass destruction (WMD) or materials had been destroyed.

UN inspectors were withdrawn from Iraq in 1998 after the Iraqi government reneged on promises to cooperate. Nevertheless, the debate on continuing the search for WMD evidence continued. On December 17, 1999, the UN Security Council passed a resolution replacing UNSCOM with UNMOVIC (the UN Monitoring, Verification, and Inspection Commission) and requesting that Iraq allow the inspectors to enter the nation and conduct unimpeded searches in exchange for the temporary suspension of economic sanctions against Iraq. Iraq refused the offer. Except for a brief inspection by IAEA in 2000, weapons inspectors did not return to Iraq until 2002.

In several meetings between March and July 2002, UN secretary-general Kofi Annan, UNMOVIC executive chairman Hans Blix, and Iraqi officials discussed arms inspections for the first time in nearly four years. However, the UN was unable to convince Iraq to readmit inspectors. Iraq did not change its mind until September 16, 2002. Perhaps not coincidentally, the nation's acquiescence occurred only four days after Bush addressed the UN General Assembly on the need for the international organization to respond to the Iraqi threat. In his speech, the president listed the promises Saddam Hussein had reneged on following Iraq's defeat in the Persian Gulf War in 1991. Saddam's failures included refusing to end human rights abuses, to dissociate his nation from terrorist groups, and to end the development of all long-range missiles and weapons of mass destruction. Bush declared that peace could be achieved if Iraq would fulfill its promises. However, in a clear expression of the Bush Doctrine, he continued, "If Iraq's regime defies us again, the world must move deliberately, decisively to hold Iraq to account. We will work with the U.N. Security Council for the necessary resolutions. But the purposes of the United States should not be doubted."[4]

Weapons inspectors returned to Iraq in November 2002. In January 2003 Blix reported that the teams had yet to find definitive proof of Iraq's WMD program, although they did discover twelve warheads that could carry chemical weapons. Discussion began in the UN Security Council on whether to extend weapons inspections in Iraq. On February 5, 2003, in a speech before the UN Security Council, Bush's secretary of state, Colin Powell, expressed the administration's view that ample proof of a WMD program existed and that war was the necessary next step. Powell offered six reasons, or "smoking guns," why the UN should support war against Iraq. According to Powell, Iraq possessed biological weapons; it owned chemical weapons; it was working to acquire nuclear weapons; it owned mobile weapon labs, where additional biological weapons could be built; it repeatedly violated international standards of human rights, including the use of ethnic cleansing and executions against the Kurds; and it had links to terrorism. Powell observed that bin Laden collaborator Abu Musab al-Zarqawi operated a terrorist network that was harbored by the Iraqi government. As the September 2002 and February 2003 speeches indicate, the Bush White House felt it was necessary to take preemptive action before Iraq could use its purported weapons or abet a terrorist attack.

Nonetheless, those speeches failed to convince the UN, including key nations such as Security Council members France, Germany, and Russia, all of whom felt it was too soon to go to war and instead called for the continuation of weapons inspections, a suggestion rejected by the United States and Great Britain. Despite receiving little support from most of Europe and the Western world, with the notable exception of Great Britain, the United States declared war on Iraq in March 2003. Unlike the Persian Gulf War of 1991, the 2003 war would not include a broad-based coalition. Nor was it intended to help a nation like Kuwait regain its sovereignty. Instead, the goal of the 2003 war was to end Saddam Hussein's regime and prevent future terrorist attacks.

Although the claim that Saddam Hussein had deadly weapons at his disposal was central to Bush's doctrine of preemption, as of July 2003 no such weapons had been found, raising debate on the legitimacy of the war and whether Americans were misled as to the threat posed by Iraq. With the ongoing and thus far fruitless search for weapons of mass destruction, the continued deaths of coalition soldiers despite the end of major combat, and audiotapes suggesting that Saddam is alive and in hiding, the decision of the Bush White House to go to war against Iraq remains controversial. In *Examining Issues Through Political Cartoons: Iraq*, the cartoonists offer a variety of perspectives on the Iraq conflict in the following chapters: Why Did the United States Go to War Against Iraq?, Perspectives on the War, The War and Its Immediate Aftermath, and The Future of Iraq. By examining these cartoons, it is hoped that the reader will have a better understanding of the debate on Iraq that was the focus of the world for more than a year.

Notes

1. George W. Bush, State of the Union address, January 29, 2002.

2. George W. Bush, commencement address at the United States Military Academy (West Point), June 1, 2002.

3. George Soros, "America's Global Role: Why the Fight for a Worldwide Open Society Begins at Home," *American Prospect*, June 2003.

4. George W. Bush, address to the United Nations General Assembly, September 12, 2002.

Chapter 1

Why Did the United States Go to War Against Iraq?

EXAMINING ISSUES THROUGH
POLITICAL CARTOONS

Preface

For many years, Saddam Hussein was considered one of the world's most dangerous figures, as the international community feared that the Iraqi leader possessed the materials required to build weapons of mass destruction. In April 1991, following Iraq's defeat in the Persian Gulf War, the UN Security Council ordered Saddam to eliminate his nation's nuclear, biological, and chemical weapons programs and destroy all long-range ballistic missiles. That demand set in motion more than eleven years of attempts to discern the true breadth of Iraq's ability to wage war. Iraq's purported arsenal was one of the reasons cited by the George W. Bush administration to justify war with Iraq in 2003.

The Iraqi government agreed to the 1991 demands, but such acquiescence was little more than lip service. As the editors of *Arms Control Today* explained in an October 2002 article: "Baghdad agreed to these conditions but for eight years deceived, obstructed, and threatened international inspectors sent to dismantle and verify the destruction of its banned programs." In December 1998, after the Iraqi government reneged on promises to cooperate, inspectors from the UN Special Commission (UNSCOM, which had been set up by the United Nations to handle the nonnuclear weapons inspections) and the International Atomic Energy Agency (IAEA) withdrew from Iraq.

UNSCOM and IAEA revealed their findings in reports issued in January and February 1999, respectively. The UNSCOM report indicated that Iraq had not been forthcoming about its nonnuclear weapons programs. The report stated that Iraq had conducted research into chemical weapons and had initially concealed the extent of its ballistic missiles program. However, the inspectors had been able to supervise the destruction of 690 tons of chemical warfare agents, 817 ballistic missiles, and 50 missile warheads. While the full breadth of Iraq's ability to build biological and chemical weapons could not be determined, IAEA concluded in February 1999 that its inspectors saw "no indication that Iraq possesse[d] nuclear weapons or any meaningful amounts of weapon-usable nuclear material." However, the committee conceded that it could not prove that no such weapons or materials existed.

In his January 2002 State of the Union address, Bush listed Iraq among the "Axis of Evil"—nations that posed a significant threat to global security. That speech sparked more than a year of debates on how best to deal with Iraq and its ability to wage war. On September 16, four days after Bush addressed the United Nations on the need for multilateral action against the Saddam Hussein regime, Iraq decided to readmit inspectors. Weapons inspections began anew two months later. On January 9, 2003, Hans Blix—chairman of the United Nations Monitoring, Verification and Inspection Commission (UNMOVIC)—stated that the inspectors had yet to find any "smoking guns" in their search for weapons of mass destruction. One week later, weapons inspectors located twelve warheads with the capability to carry chemical weapons. In early February, U.S. secretary of state Colin Powell presented a report to the UN detailing evidence of Iraq's weapons program. Toward the end of the month, UN Security Council members France, Germany, and Russia called for a four-month extension of weapons inspections, a proposal spurned by the United States and Great Britain. On March 20, 2003, despite being unable to convince the Security Council to turn away from inspections and instead endorse the use of force against Iraq, coalition forces started their military campaign.

The purported ability of Saddam Hussein to use deadly weapons against his enemies was one of the reasons the United States, Britain, and other coalition forces went to war against Iraq. In this chapter the cartoonists evaluate the arguments offered by the Bush administration in favor of war. As their drawings suggest, not everyone believed that Iraq's possession of weapons of mass destruction was the true motive behind the decision to attack Iraq.

Examining Cartoon 1:
"This Evil Man Poses the Greatest Threat"

About the Cartoon

In this cartoon Tom Tomorrow suggests that President George W. Bush decided to pursue war against Iraq and its leader, Saddam Hussein, as a way of deflecting attention from his failure to find terrorist mastermind Osama bin Laden. In the first frame Bush is pointing to a picture of bin Laden, the man behind the September 11, 2001, terrorist attacks, and declaring that the terrorist must be found because he poses the greatest threat to the United States. However, the president is interrupted by a military leader who in the second frame lets Bush know that bin Laden has not been found and suggests that Bush might want to change his tactics before the 2002 midterm elections. Bush disappears behind a curtain in the third frame. In the fourth panel Bush reemerges, this time with a photo of Saddam, and repeats the words he uttered in the first frame. Bush further separates himself from the hunt for bin Laden in the final panel, when he expresses ignorance about bin Laden after being questioned by Sparky the Penguin (a recurring character in Tomorrow's cartoons). Bush associates bin Laden with Enron, a large energy corporation that collapsed amid controversial circumstances, another political issue many people believe Bush has largely ignored. By using the images in these five frames, Tomorrow appears to be arguing that the president's decision to focus on Saddam rather than bin Laden was a political move, one prompted by Bush's concern that Democratic candidates would use the failure to find bin Laden as a campaign issue during the 2002 midterm elections. Instead of continuing an as-yet-unsuccessful search for bin Laden, Tomorrow contends that Bush chose to face an easier target in Iraq in order to appear a more successful leader.

About the Cartoonist

Tom Tomorrow (real name Dan Perkins) draws the weekly cartoon *This Modern World*, which is published in 150 newspapers and magazines. Among Perkins's awards are the 1998 Robert F. Kennedy Journalism Award for Cartooning, the Media Alliance Meritorious Achievement Award for Excellence in Journalism, and the Society of Professional Journalists' James Madison Freedom of Information Award. Six collections of *This Modern World* have been printed, including *When Penguins Attack* and *Penguin Soup for the Soul*.

Examining Cartoon 2:
"I Have Six Smoking Guns"

About the Cartoon

People and organizations opposed to the war in Iraq frequently asserted that President George W. Bush and his administration had no concrete evidence that Iraq posed a threat to worldwide security. In this cartoon Gary Varvel suggests that the White House had six valid reasons to pursue war against Iraqi leader Saddam Hussein's regime. Varvel's drawing refers directly to a report Secretary of State Colin Powell presented on February 5, 2003, before the United Nations Security Council, three months after UN inspectors began searching Iraq for weapons of mass destruction.

Powell offered six reasons—portrayed by Varvel as "smoking guns" —in support of war. The first reason was biological weapons: According to Powell, sources had indicated that Iraq had a missile brigade located outside the capital city of Baghdad, from where warheads and rocket launchers containing biological warfare agents could be distributed throughout the country. Powell stated that the biological agents produced by Iraq included anthrax, ricin, aflatoxin, and botulinum toxin and added that the Iraqi regime had investigated methods of dispersing these deadly agents. The secretary of state reported that Iraq posed a nuclear threat (the second smoking gun), telling the United Nations that there was more than a decade of proof that Saddam was trying to acquire nuclear weapons. According to Powell, "Saddam Hussein already possesses two out of the three key components needed to build a nuclear bomb. He has a cadre of nuclear scientists with the expertise, and he has a bomb design." The remaining step for Iraq was acquiring fissionable material, most likely by learning how to enrich uranium. Powell detailed the variety of steps taken by Saddam to acquire such material, including attempting to acquire aluminum tubes that are used during the enrichment process. He also alleged that Iraq was trying to hide evidence of ballistic missiles. The third justification for war was Iraq's possession of chemical weapons. Powell asserted that Iraq had a weapons facility that housed chemical munitions and that vast quantities of chemical weapons had not been accounted for. The weapons included VX, which can kill within minutes if a drop is applied to skin. The UN weapons inspectors, according to the report, had evidence that Iraq possessed VX. The fourth reason given by Powell was the existence, confirmed in 2000, of mobile weapons labs located on trucks and train cars, where biological weapons could be built. According to Varvel, Powell's report proved that Iraq posed a serious threat to world security and that it had failed to destroy its biological, chemical, and nuclear weapons programs as had been demanded by the United Nations.

However, as Varvel's cartoon suggests, weapons were not Powell's sole justification for war. The final two smoking guns concerned Iraq's human rights violations and ties to terrorists. The secretary of state cited several examples of Iraq's horrible human rights record, including the use of mustard gas on the Kurds, a non-Arab minority that lives in northeastern Iraq. He further pointed out that the Kurds suffered ethnic cleansing, executions, jailings, and disappearances. Another minority that was mistreated under Saddam were the Shia Iraqis, who follow the Shiite path of Islam and were also subjected to ethnic cleansing. The final smoking gun shown in Varvel's cartoon is the link between Iraq and terrorism. Powell pointed out that Hussein's regime had funded Palestinian terrorists and given money to the families of suicide bombers. He also asserted that Iraq was linked to the al-Qaeda terrorist network because Iraq harbored a terrorist network operated by Abu Musab Al-Zarqawi, a collaborator of al-Qaeda leader Osama bin Laden, who could conduct terrorist attacks throughout the world from his posts in Iraq. In addition, he reported that members of al-Qaeda and Iraq's government had met at least eight times. Powell's report, Varvel suggests, clearly counters any arguments against going to war with Iraq.

About the Cartoonist

Gary Varvel has been the editorial cartoonist for the *Indianapolis Star* since 1994. He has published a collection of his work, *Varvelous*.

Examining Cartoon 3:
"Our Doctrine of Preemption at Work!"

About the Cartoon

Early in his presidency, George W. Bush adopted a doctrine of pre-emption, which held that military action was justified against nations that posed a threat to U.S. security, even if those nations had not yet attacked. Matt Wuerker suggests in this cartoon that the Bush White House—represented by President George W. Bush and Vice President Dick Cheney in military marching garb—is employing the doctrine of preemption to preempt discussion of America's domestic problems. The leaders' repeated cry to "attack Iraq" is drowning out the voices of citizens who are attempting to address other issues. The problems Wuerker believes are being ignored by the Bush administration include the struggling U.S. economy and the failure of Congress to pass legislation that would make prescription drugs affordable. He also targets the American educational system, which many people have argued is overcrowded and underfunded. Another problem Wuerker alludes to is the Enron scandal, the collapse of an energy company that cost thousands of employees their jobs and pensions and debilitated the stock market.

About the Cartoonist

Matt Wuerker draws the weekly cartoon *Lint Trap*, which appears in such publications as *Z Magazine*, *Christian Science Monitor*, and the *Philadelphia Daily News*.

Examining Cartoon 4:
War For Weapons or Oil?

About the Cartoon

In this cartoon Jean Plantu points out the disparity in the policy of President George W. Bush toward Iraq and North Korea. North Korea, depicted in the person of its dictator Kim Jong Il sitting on a warhead, sticking out his tongue and thumbing his nose at Bush, has admitted to building nuclear weapons in violation of a treaty brokered with the United States in 1994. Despite those aggressive actions toward the United States, the president has expressed no plans to take action against North Korea. On the other hand, the United States was eager to attack Iraq even though there was no definitive proof that Iraq possessed the materials needed to build weapons of mass destruction.

By drawing Iraqi leader Saddam Hussein next to an oil derrick, Plantu suggests that the real reason Bush wanted to go to war against Iraq was so American oil companies could gain control of that country's oil fields. Plantu's drawing of Bush flying on a missile further suggests that the cartoonist believes the president is a warmonger, as the image is reminiscent of Stanley Kubrick's satirical film *Dr. Strangelove*, in which the war-crazy character of Major T. J. "King" Kong rides on the nuclear bomb that sends the world into Armageddon.

About the Cartoonist

Jean Plantu has been the editorial cartoonist for *Le Monde*, France's leading daily newspaper, since 1972.

Chapter 2

Perspectives on the War

EXAMINING ISSUES THROUGH
POLITICAL CARTOONS

Preface

Many people turn to sports as a way of taking their minds off war. In the 2003 conflict against Iraq, however, sports and war collided in a controversy that helped typify the debate over the limits of free speech when America is at war. The cancellation of a screening of the popular baseball movie *Bull Durham* by U.S. Baseball Hall of Fame president Dale Petroskey led to a nearly two-week-long controversy and numerous opinion pieces in sports and editorial pages.

The Hall of Fame had scheduled an April 2003 tribute to *Bull Durham*, featuring appearances by its director Ron Shelton and stars Tim Robbins and Susan Sarandon. However, in an April 7, 2003, letter addressed to Robbins, Petroskey canceled the screening out of concern that the actors—who had spoken out frequently against the war in Iraq—would use the Hall of Fame event for political purposes. Petroskey explained, "We believe your very public criticism of President Bush at this important—and sensitive—time in our nation's history helps undermine the US position, which ultimately could put our troops in even more danger."

Robbins fired back two days later. In his response to the hall's president, the actor wrote that he had been looking forward to a weekend away from politics and war and expressed his dismay that baseball had become politicized. Robbins added that although he had not intended to discuss the war at the Hall of Fame event, "As an American who believes that vigorous debate is necessary for the survival of a democracy, I reject your suggestion that one must be silent in time of war. To suggest that my criticism of the President puts the troops in danger is absurd. If people had listened to that twisted logic we'd still be in Vietnam."

31

Robbins's defense of his right to free speech did not receive universal support. Bobby Eberle, the president of GOPUSA, a news and commentary organization, wrote in *Insight on the News:* "Robbins, like many on the liberal left, just doesn't get it. For him, it is perfectly fine to exercise his First Amendment rights to criticize the war with Iraq . . . just as long as he is not criticized in return." Eberle further suggested that Robbins and Sarandon would have, despite Robbins's claims to the contrary, made political statements at the *Bull Durham* tribute.

Petroskey apologized for his actions on April 18, explaining that he should have discussed his decision with the actors before making it public. However, he did not apologize directly to Robbins or Sarandon, nor did he reinstate the event.

Tim Robbins and Susan Sarandon are not the only people with controversial views on the war. In this chapter the cartoonists present their thoughts on domestic and international attitudes toward the war in Iraq. While the military battles might have been fought thousands of miles from America, the battle for public opinion was held much closer to home.

Examining Cartoon 1:
"Bush Is Talking Like We Don't Even Exist!"

About the Cartoon

In the days and weeks leading up to the war in Iraq, large protests took place in Washington, D.C., and other cities. However, these protests seemed to have no effect on the decision-making of President George W. Bush, who forged ahead with preparations and increased the intensity of his rhetoric in speeches to the nation and the United Nations. This cartoon captures the frustration of protesters who feel that their message is going unheeded by the president. It also emphasizes Bush's single-mindedness in going to war in Iraq by presenting Osama bin Laden, formerly the main target in America's War on Terrorism, as simply another neglected protester.

About the Cartoonist

Rob Rogers has been the editorial cartoonist for the *Pittsburgh Post-Gazette* since 1993; his works have also appeared regularly in *Newsweek*, *USA Today*, the *New York Times*, and other publications. Rogers' cartoons have received a number of honors, including seven Golden Quills, the 1995 National Headliner Award, and the 2000 Overseas Press Club Award.

Examining Cartoon 2:
"Anti-War Protestors Only Make Him Smile"

About the Cartoon

Prior to the U.S.-led attack on Iraq, protesters took to the streets worldwide to oppose the impending military action. In this cartoon Gary Varvel argues that antiwar protestors are actually supporting Iraqi dictator Saddam Hussein's deadly regime. Varvel depicts Saddam in a hat emblazoned with a skull, an indication of the leader's violence toward his subjects. Among the atrocities committed by Saddam and his cohorts were torture, chemical attacks, the raping and beheading of women, and the diversion of food supplies intended for starving Iraqis. Hundreds of thousands of Iraqis and Kurds were killed under his rule. Varvel's cartoon suggests that the only way to end Saddam's brutality is by overthrowing the Iraqi government.

About the Cartoonist

Gary Varvel has been the editorial cartoonist for the *Indianapolis Star* since 1994. He has published a collection of his work, *Varvelous.*

Examining Cartoon 3:
"I Can't See a Reason to Go to War with Iraq"

"I can't see a reason to go to war with Iraq. . . . "

About the Cartoon

One of the nations that most strongly opposed the decision to go to war against Iraq was France. Michael Ramirez questions France's reasons for protesting the war in this cartoon. He portrays French president Jacques Chirac looking into a pair of binoculars featuring lenses shaped like oil barrels and the label "Iraqi Oil Contracts." By using that image, Ramirez is suggesting that France does not support the war because the nation does not want to lose the valuable oil contracts it signed during Saddam Hussein's rule. A change in regime could lead to the cancellation of those contracts, thus costing France billions of dollars and further damaging its weak economy. In addition, according to reports by Iraqi defectors, Saddam and his sons used kickbacks from those contracts to purchase military supplies from France—further indicating the hypocrisy of France's antiwar stance.

About the Cartoonist

Michael Ramirez is the editorial cartoonist for the *Los Angeles Times* and the winner of the 1994 Pulitzer Prize for editorial cartooning.

Chapter 3

The War and Its Immediate Aftermath

EXAMINING ISSUES THROUGH
POLITICAL CARTOONS

Preface

For journalists, few assignments are more thrilling—or more dangerous—than covering wars. Legendary World War II correspondent Ernie Pyle was killed by a Japanese sniper in 1945, while sixty-four journalists lost their lives during the decade-long Vietnam War. The spring 2003 war in Iraq proved to be the deadliest war for the media since Vietnam, with eleven print, television, and radio employees dying in the three weeks prior to the overthrow of Baghdad. The fatalities included NBC correspondent David Bloom, former *Atlantic Monthly* editor Michael Kelly, and ITN reporter Terry Lloyd. While all the deaths were tragic, three proved particularly controversial. The worldwide press and several international journalist organizations excoriated the Pentagon after two incidents on April 8, 2003, led to the deaths of Ukrainian cameraman Taras Protsyuk, Spanish cameraman Jose Couso, and Palestinian television reporter Tareq Ayoub.

The first two men died when the hotel where they were based, Baghdad's Palestine Hotel, was fired on by a U.S. tank. U.S. military commanders said the tank had been ordered to fire as a response to snipers who had been shooting from the building. In the second incident, Ayoub, a correspondent for the Arabic television network al Jazeera, died when an American bomb hit al Jazeera's Baghdad bureau. Once again, the Pentagon contended that the strike occurred after "significant enemy fire" was reported to have come from Ayoub's office.

Thirteen days later, in response to the events at the Palestine Hotel, U.S. secretary of state Colin Powell wrote a letter to the Spanish foreign minister in which he defended the American troops' actions. Powell contended, "The use of force was justified and the amount of force was proportionate to the threat against United States forces."

Powell's letter was not universally supported. The Committee to Protect Journalists (CPJ)—an organization that defends the right of journalists to report news without worrying about reprisal—questioned Powell's defense, in a report issued on May 28, 2003. Journalists based in the Palestine Hotel, according to the report, saw no proof that people had been shooting from the hotel. CPJ wrote, "There is simply no evidence to support the official U.S. position that U.S. forces were returning hostile fire from the Palestine Hotel. It conflicts with the eyewitness testimony of numerous journalists in the hotel." In addition, the report adds that while senior Pentagon officials were aware that the hotel was filled with journalists, the military "failed to convey their concern to the tank commander who fired on the hotel." While CPJ did not believe the attack was intentional, another organization, Reporters Without Borders, accused the military of deliberately firing upon the journalists and requested Secretary of Defense Donald Rumsfeld prove that American troops were acting in self-defense. Couso's family filed a lawsuit against three American soldiers involved in the Palestine Hotel incident, charging them with war crimes for using excessive force against civilians. The deaths of the three journalists are likely to remain controversial for a long time.

War is a danger not only to soldiers but also to civilians, as the deaths of journalists based in Iraq proved. The cartoonists in this chapter examine life in Iraq for those who were directly involved in the war, the men and women reporting on the battles, and Iraq's noncombatant citizens.

Examining Cartoon 1:
"The Brass Insist You Wear the Mask"

About the Cartoon

During the 2003 war against Iraq, hundreds of journalists lived and worked alongside soldiers. These television, radio, and print reporters believed that such proximity would lead to more complete coverage of the war and bring their audiences closer to the action—especially when compared to the censored coverage of the 1991 Persian Gulf War, when all photos and reports had to be approved by censors before they could be published or broadcast. In this cartoon Larry Wright argues that despite their hopes, these "embedded" journalists were themselves censored by the military. The dialogue between the two soldiers and the journalist indicates that the military leadership did not want Americans to be aware of any "dangerous germs"—stories that might indicate that the war was not going as well as its supporters believed. As the comments of the second soldier indicate, safety was another reason for wartime censorship—the U.S. military did not want to put its soldiers at risk by having journalists publish their exact locations or military strategies. By showing the reporter in a mask, Wright is also making a visual pun on the deadly epidemic Severe Acute Respiratory Syndrome (SARS), another issue that garnered worldwide attention in spring 2003. People fearful of falling ill in high-risk areas such as China took to wearing masks in order to avoid inhaling deadly germs. By June 2003 the flu-like disease had killed more than seven hundred people in China, Hong Kong, and Canada.

About the Cartoonist

Larry Wright has been the editorial cartoonist for the *Detroit News* since 1976. He also draws the comic strip *Kit 'n' Carlyle* and is a past president of the Association of American Editorial Cartoonists.

Wright. © 2003 by Larry Wright. Reprinted by permission of Cagle Cartoons, Inc., www.caglecartoons.com.

Examining Cartoon 2:
"al CNN"

About the Cartoon

In this cartoon Peter Steiner appears to compare American news network CNN with an Arabic counterpart, al Jazeera. Supporters of the war were highly critical of al Jazeera, contending that the network has a history of anti-American bias and is too willing to allow terrorists to broadcast their views—for example, the station has aired speeches by Osama bin Laden and his al-Qaeda compatriots. In Steiner's opinion CNN may also be prejudiced against the United States.

A confession by CNN's chief news executive Eason Jordan likely inspired Steiner's cartoon. In April 2003 Jordan admitted in a *New York Times* column that the network repeatedly decided against airing reports on the brutality of Iraqi leader Saddam Hussein and his sons because the network feared that the Iraqis who had provided information on the atrocities would be tortured and killed by the Iraqi government. Political commentators castigated Jordan for his remarks, charging that CNN's silence helped Saddam's regime remain in power and alleging that the network's reports during the war could not be fully trusted because information might have been omitted.

About the Cartoonist

Peter Steiner is a cartoonist for the *Washington Times* and the *Weekly Standard*.

Examining Cartoon 3:
"Change the Channel"

About the Cartoon

In this cartoon, Daryl Cagle pokes fun at the attitudes of Arab observers of the war in Iraq. He shows a couple watching the news following the entrance of the coalition troops into Baghdad. On April 9, 2003, Iraqi citizens rejoiced as they toppled a giant statue of Iraqi dictator Saddam Hussein, and networks around the world aired the footage of the symbolic overthrow. Cagle suggests that the couple in his cartoon are displeased by such prowar coverage and would rather watch stations that present an anti-American take on the war—one that emphasizes (and possibly exaggerates) the number of civilian casualties and ignores the way Iraqi lives will improve after the downfall of the Saddam Hussein regime.

About the Cartoonist

Daryl Cagle is the political cartoonist of the online magazine Slate.com. He also posts cartoons from around the United States and the world on his page at http://cagle.slate.msn.com.

Examining Cartoon 4:
"Nobody Told Me You Were Gonna Fight Back"

About the Cartoon

Many of the people who supported the war against Iraq in 2003 believed that the Iraqi army would be no match for American troops, who had handily defeated Iraq in 1991 during the Persian Gulf War. However, as Brian Fairrington indicates in this cartoon, Iraqi resistance proved to be a surprisingly powerful force. He depicts a medal-emblazoned Uncle Sam, symbol of the United States, whose hat has been shot off by a powerful Iraqi weapon. Uncle Sam is surprised that his toy gun was not sufficient to overcome Iraq, and his words suggest he underestimated the Iraqi response to the coalition invasion. Examples of Iraqi resistance included an Iraqi attack in Nasiriya that left two dozen American soldiers dead and fifty wounded and an attack on thirty-two Apache helicopters that had been attacking a tank brigade; the pilots had to withdraw. Coalition forces were also unable to dislodge Iraqi soldiers in Umm Qasr, despite having superior weapons. American soldiers continued to face resistance even after major combat ended in May.

About the Cartoonist

Brian Fairrington is a cartoonist for the *Arizona Republic*. As an editorial cartoonist for his college newspaper, Fairrington won a number of major awards, including the Association of American Editorial Cartoonist's John Locher Memorial Award and the Charles Schulz Award from the Scripps Howard Foundation.

Fairrington. © 2003 by *Arizona Republic*. Reprinted by permission of Cagle Cartoons, Inc., www.cagle cartoons.com.

Examining Cartoon 5:
"Freedom's Just Another Word"

About the Cartoon

Iraqis were eager to experience freedom after the fall of Baghdad and the overthrow of Saddam Hussein's regime. However, as this cartoon by David Horsey suggests, this newfound freedom had unfortunate consequences. Iraqis looted much of Baghdad, including the former palaces of Saddam and his family. Unfortunately, they also ransacked the National Museum of Iraq, where relics from the world's earliest civilization, which had been founded in the ancient Iraqi region of Mesopotamia, were housed. The priceless artifacts included prehistoric tools, one of the first wheels, pottery, and clay tablets. Archaeologists and museum curators considered the theft and destruction of much of the museum's collections a tragedy, and the American government and military leaders were criticized for failing to guard the museum. However, it was later discovered that only thirty-eight pieces were missing, not tens of thousands of artifacts as earlier reported.

In this cartoon, drawn prior to that discovery, David Horsey depicts two Iraqis watching the looting and lamenting the destruction of the museum. The first man points out the failure of coalition troops to protect the museum and wonders if Iraq's new freedom can make up for the loss of seven thousand years of history. His friend, who holds a broken vase in his hands, quotes from the popular song "Me and Bobby McGee," written by Kris Kristofferson and made famous by 1960s singer Janis Joplin, as a way of explaining the American attitude toward freedom.

About the Cartoonist

David Horsey, a two-time Pulitzer Prize winner for editorial cartoons, is the political cartoonist for the *Seattle Post-Intelligencer*. He is a past president of the Association of American Editorial Cartoonists and has published four anthologies of his work, including 1999's *One Man Show*.

Chapter 4

The Future of Iraq

Preface

The overthrow of Saddam Hussein by coalition forces will almost certainly change the lives of millions of Iraqis. Groups that had been oppressed under his violent regime, such as Shiite Muslims, are likely to gain political power. One segment of the Iraqi population that may also enjoy new opportunities is its women. However, it is still too soon to tell whether the fall of Baghdad will result in freedom for all Iraqis or if political and social rights will continue to be ignored.

Until 1991 Iraqi women were perhaps the most privileged of all Middle Eastern women. They had the right to work, attend school, and vote and held as much as 20 percent of the seats in Iraq's parliament. A constitution implemented in 1970 made Iraqi men and women equal under the law. Working mothers received an incredible five years of maternity leave.

The good fortune of Iraqi women ended after their nation was defeated in the first Gulf War in 1991. Economic sanctions applied by the United Nations led to a sharp rise in the unemployment rate. Numerous Iraqi women lost their jobs and began to abandon their education, resulting in a decrease in female literacy. More troubling for women was the increasing turn of Saddam Hussein's government toward laws that almost completely eliminated their human rights. Women could be sentenced to death for a variety of offenses, such as committing adultery, fighting with their husbands, or being raped (because that crime is considered by certain Islamic sects to bring shame upon the family). Under Iraqi law a man who killed a female relative in order to protect the family's honor would not be punished.

Torture and rape were two more tools of the Saddam regime. The U.S. Department of State's Bureau of Public Affairs notes in its report "Women in Iraq" that Saddam's regime used rape to extract confessions and information from the women's detained relatives and intimidated political opponents by sending them videotapes of the rapes of female relatives. According to the report, "Saddam Hussein's thugs [also] routinely tortured and killed female dissidents and the female relatives of Iraqi oppositionists and defectors."

With all the horrors Iraqi women faced for a dozen years, one might think that they were relieved when the Saddam regime was toppled following the coalition victory in spring 2003. However, as Iraq begins its rebuilding process, many Iraqi women and international observers worry that Iraq's females face two threats: Not only are Iraqi women being shut out of the formation of a new government, but the new regime might further destroy women's rights. Laura Liswood, writing for the *Christian Science Monitor*, points out that only five of the thirty members of the Iraqi Reconstruction Group, an organization that supports the establishment of a democratic government and works to rebuild Iraq's infrastructure, are women. She adds that no women were included in the panel of thirteen legal experts, assembled by the U.S. Justice Department to rebuild Iraq's court system. According to Liswood, if the reconstructed government is dominated by fundamentalist Shiite Muslims, "Women could be denied the opportunity to learn, have access to healthcare, speak in public, hold political office, and participate in the economy. The United States would win the battle and lose any hope for a thriving democracy." John Daniszewski, in a report in the June 1, 2003, edition of the *Los Angeles Times*, writes that Shiite militants have already begun opening Islamic courts, posting rules of behavior in schools, and demanding that Iraqi women wear traditional Muslim head coverings.

The future of Iraq and its women will likely not be fully known for many years. In this chapter the cartoonists offer their views on the reconstruction of Iraq. While the war in Iraq may have freed the Iraqis from a despotic tyrant, the coalition success does not necessarily guarantee permanent peace and freedom.

Examining Cartoon 1:
"Yankee Go Home!"

About the Cartoon

Steven Breen pokes fun at the ambivalent attitudes the Iraqi people have shown toward the U.S. presence in Iraq. Soon after the U.S.-led coalition ousted Saddam Hussein's regime, many Iraqi people began to demand the departure of American troops. Having lived under Saddam's control for more than twenty years, Iraqis may have feared a lengthy period of U.S. rule. However, as Breen points out in this cartoon, these Iraqis did not want the United States to leave until it had restored order and security and rebuilt the war-torn nation's infrastructure. The cartoon implies that Iraqis are ungrateful for the assistance they are receiving.

About the Cartoonist

Steven Breen has been the editorial cartoonist for the *San Diego Union-Tribune* since 2001. In 1998 he won the Pulitzer Prize for editorial cartooning for his work at the *Asbury Park Press*. His editorial cartoons have appeared in the *New York Times, Newsweek,* and *USA Today*. Breen also draws the daily comic strip *Grand Avenue*, which appears in more than one hundred newspapers.

Examining Cartoon 2:
"Uh-Oh"

About the Cartoon

On April 9, 2003, Iraqi civilians—with the help of coalition soldiers—toppled a gigantic statue of Saddam Hussein, symbolically ending the dictator's long and deadly regime. The celebration in the Baghdad square was viewed by millions of people worldwide. Mike Luckovich suggests in this cartoon that while the Iraqis were delighted by the literal and figurative fall of Saddam, their joy might be short-lived. A military helicopter places a statue of "Rummy," or Secretary of Defense Donald Rumsfeld, in the spot where the Saddam statue had stood. Luckovich is implying that the conservative cabinet member's plans for rebuilding Iraq may not leave Iraqis any better off than they were before. The Rumsfeld blueprint, which denies the United Nations a substantial role in the reconstruction process and outlines an indefinite period of U.S. military rule, was widely criticized in the worldwide press. Rumsfeld had also insisted—contrary to statements made by National Security Adviser Condoleezza Rice—that only the Iraqis who had been exiled by Saddam and had returned to southern Iraq after the war would head the Iraqi Interim Authority, which would take over some government duties and have the authority to collect and spend Iraqi oil revenue. Although as of June 2003 it was unclear what shape the future Iraqi government would take, in Luckovich's opinion the end of the Saddam Hussein regime may lead to another government that also limits the freedoms of Iraqis.

About the Cartoonist

Mike Luckovich is the editorial cartoonist for the *Atlanta Journal-Constitution*. Luckovich, who won the Pulitzer Prize for editorial cartooning in 1995, is syndicated in a number of papers and magazines, among them *Time, Newsweek,* and the *Washington Post. Lotsa Luckovich* is a collection of his cartoons.

Examining Cartoon 3:

"I've Invited My United Nations Friends"

About the Cartoon

The United States' decision to go to war against Iraq was not widely supported by the United Nations. France, Germany, and Russia were the most vocal opponents at the UN, using their power as members of the UN Security Council to block resolutions that would authorize the use of force in Iraq. By comparison Great Britain was America's staunchest ally, with its military heavily involved in the war.

With this cartoon Daryl Cagle depicts British prime minister Tony Blair telling President George W. Bush that the UN should participate in rebuilding Iraq. Cagle's drawing indicates his opposition to the idea by presenting the members of the UN as the devil, Dracula, Frankenstein, a rat, and a chimpanzee. The chimpanzee, wearing a beret and striped shirt, symbolizes France.

About the Cartoonist

Daryl Cagle is the cartoonist for the Web magazine *Slate.com*. He also hosts the work of other cartoonists at http://cagle.slate.msn.com

Examining Cartoon 4:
"Rumsfeld's Iraq Victory Dance"

About the Cartoon

In this cartoon David Horsey suggest that U.S. secretary of defense Donald Rumsfeld was too quick to gloat over America's victory against Iraq. A spear-wielding Rumsfeld is depicted as dancing triumphantly, only to find himself outnumbered by Islamic fundamentalists who are cheerfully dancing the cancan. This cartoon points at the anti-American attitudes that sprouted in Iraq after coalition forces declared victory against Saddam Hussein's regime, as well as the role that might be played by Iraq's Muslim population. For example, a prominent Sunni Muslim cleric called for a religious war against American soldiers based in Iraq. Shiite Muslims, who despite making up 60 percent of the population were oppressed under Saddam Hussein's Sunni-dominated government, have disagreed among themselves whether Iraq's new government should be secular or model the theocracy of Iran, another heavily Shiite nation. While the United States is opposed to the formation of an Iraqi government dominated by religious leaders, this cartoon suggests that America's authority in Iraq may be short-lived.

About the Cartoonist

David Horsey, a two-time Pulitzer Prize winner for editorial cartoons, is the political cartoonist for the *Seattle Post-Intelligencer*. He is a past president of the Association of American Editorial Cartoonists and has published four anthologies of his work, including 1999's *One Man Show*.

Organizations to Contact

The editors have compiled the following list of organizations concerned with the issues debated in this book. The descriptions are derived from materials provided by the organizations. All have publications or information available for interested readers. This list was compiled on the date of publication of the present volume; the information provided here may change. Be aware that many organizations take several weeks or longer to respond to inquiries, so allow as much time as possible.

Iraq Action Coalition
7309 Haymarket Ln., Raleigh, NC 27615
fax: (919) 846-7422 (cover page required)
e-mail: IAC@leb.net • website: www.iraqaction.org

The Iraq Action Coalition is an online resource center for groups and activists who are opposed to the war in Iraq. The website offers publications and videos on Iraq, along with links to newspapers and magazine articles.

Middle East Forum
1500 Walnut St., Suite 1050, Philadelphia, PA 19102
(215) 546-5406 • fax: (215) 546-5409
e-mail: info@meforum.org • website: www.meforum.org

The Middle East Forum is a think tank that works to define and promote American interests in the Middle East. It supports strong American ties with Israel, Turkey, and other democracies as they emerge. It publishes the *Middle East Quarterly*, a policy-oriented journal. Its website includes articles on the war in Iraq, summaries of activities, and a discussion forum.

Middle East Institute
1761 N St. NW, Washington, DC 20036-2882
(202) 785-1141 • fax: (202) 331-8861
e-mail: mideasti@mideasti.org
website: www.themiddleeastinstitute.org

The institute's charter mission is to promote better understanding of Middle Eastern cultures, languages, religions, and politics. It publishes numerous books, papers, audiotapes, and videos as well as the quarterly *Middle East Journal*. It also maintains an Educational Outreach Department to give teachers and students of all grade levels advice on resources. The website provides links to articles and speeches on the war in Iraq.

Middle East Media Research Institute (MEMRI)
PO Box 27837, Washington, DC 20038-7837
(202) 955-9070 • fax: (202) 955-9077
e-mail: memri@memri.org • website: www.memri.org

MEMRI translates and disseminates articles and commentaries from Middle East media sources and provides analysis on the political, ideological, intellectual, social, cultural, and religious trends in the region. The website also features special reports and analyses on Iraq, such as "Arab and Muslim Media Reactions to the Fall of Baghdad."

Middle East Policy Council
1730 M St. NW, Suite 512, Washington, DC 20036-4505
(202) 296-6767 • fax: (202) 296-5791
e-mail: info@mepc.org • website: www.mepc.org

The Middle East Policy Council was founded in 1981 to expand public discussion and understanding of issues affecting U.S. policy in the Middle East. The council is a nonprofit educational organization that operates nationwide. It publishes the quarterly *Middle East Policy Journal* and provides links to articles about Iraq.

Middle East Research and Information Project (MERIP)
1500 Massachusetts Ave. NW, Washington, DC 20005
(202) 223-3677 • fax: (202) 223-3604
website: www.merip.org

MERIP is a nonprofit, nongovernmental organization with no links to any religious, educational, or political organizations in the United States or elsewhere. Its mission is to educate the public about the contemporary Middle East with particular emphasis on U.S. foreign policy, human rights, and social justice issues. It publishes articles and a backgrounder on Iraq, along with the bimonthly *Middle East Report*.

Target Iraq
300 N. Washington St., B-100, Alexandria, VA 22314
(703) 548-2700 • fax: (703) 548-2424
e-mail: info@globalsecurity.org
website: www.globalsecurity.org

Target Iraq is a project of Globalsecurity.org, an organization that aims to reduce the use of nuclear weapons and improve the capabilities of America's military and intelligence organizations. The website features numerous links and news and analysis on the war in Iraq and its aftermath, with a focus on Iraqi weapons and the reconstruction efforts.

United States Department of State, Bureau of Near Eastern Affairs
U.S. Department of State
2201 C St. NW, Washington, DC 20520
(202) 647-4000
website: www.state.gov/p/nea

The bureau deals with U.S. foreign policy and U.S. relations with the countries in the Middle East and North Africa, including Iraq. Its website offers country information as well as news briefings and press statements on U.S. foreign policy.

Washington Institute for Near East Policy
1828 L St. NW, Suite 1050, Washington, DC 20036
(202) 452-0650 • fax: (202) 223-5364
e-mail: info@washingtoninstitute.org
website: www.washingtoninstitute.org

The institute is an independent, nonprofit research organization that provides information and analysis on the Middle East and U.S. policy in the region. It publishes numerous books, periodic monographs, and reports on regional politics, security, and economics, including *PeaceWatch*, which focuses on the Arab-Israeli peace process, and the reports including *Democracy and Arab Political Culture* and *Radical Middle East States and U.S. Policy*. The website offers a "Focus on Iraq" section, with an archive of articles, op-eds, books, and analyses.

Websites

Patriots for the Defense of America
www.defenseofamerica.org

Patriots for the Defense of America is an organization that believes the United States must defend itself against Iraq and other enemy nations. It supports the use of military force and seeks to educate the American public on the importance of patriotism and the danger of statism. Resources provided on the website include news, analysis, articles, and editorials.

United for Peace
(212) 603-3700
www.unitedforpeace.org

United for Peace is a national antiwar campaign consisting of more than seventy peace and justice organizations. The website provides articles and commentary on the conflict in Iraq, including "Why the Anti-War Movement Was Right" and "The Case Against War."

For Further Research

Books

Saïd K. Aburish, *Saddam Hussein: The Politics of Revenge*. New York: Bloomsbury, 2000.

Anthony Arnove, ed., *Iraq Under Siege: The Deadly Impact of Sanctions and War*. Boston: South End Press, 2003.

Henry T. Azzam, *The Arab World Facing the Challenge of the New Millennium*. London: IB Tauris, 2002.

Shyam Batia and Daniel McGrory, *Brighter than the Baghdad Sun: Saddam Hussein's Nuclear Threat to the United States*. Washington, DC: Regnery, 2000.

Patrick Clawson, ed., *How to Build a New Iraq After Saddam*. Washington, DC: Washington Institute for Near East Policy, 2002.

Andrew Cockburn and Patrick Cockburn, *Out of the Ashes: The Resurrection of Saddam Hussein*. New York: HarperCollins, 1999.

Con Coughlin, *Saddam: King of Terror*. New York: Ecco, 2002.

Christopher Hitchens, *The Long Short War: The Postponed Liberation of Iraq*. New York: Plume, 2003.

Shams Inati, *Iraq: Its History, People, and Politics*. Amherst, NY: Humanity Books, 2003.

William Kristol and Lawrence Kaplan, *The War over Iraq: Saddam's Tyranny and America's Mission*. San Francisco: Encounter Books, 2003.

Juman Kubba, *The First Evidence: A Memoir of Life in Iraq Under Saddam Hussein*. Jefferson, NC: McFarland, 2003.

Joe Laredo, *Living and Working in the Middle East*. London: Survival, 2002.

Bernard Lewis, *What Went Wrong: Western Impact and Middle Eastern Response*. Oxford, UK: Oxford University Press, 2001.

Sandra Mackey, *The Reckoning: Iraq and the Legacy of Saddam Hussein*. New York: W.W. Norton, 2002.

David McDowall, *A Modern History of the Kurds*. London: IB Tauris, 2001.

John Miller and Aaron Kenedi, eds., *Inside Iraq: The History, the People, and the Politics of the World's Least Understood Land*. New York: Marlowe, 2002.

Tim Niblock, *"Pariah States" and Sanctions in the Middle East: Iraq, Libya, Sudan*. Boulder, CO: Lynne Rienner, 2002.

Micah L. Sifry and Christopher Cerf, eds., *The Iraq War Reader: History, Documents, Opinions*. New York: Touchstone Books, 2003.

Geoff Simons, *Targeting Iraq: Sanctions and Bombing in US Policy*. London: Saqi Books, 2002.

Norman Solomon et al., *Target Iraq: What the News Media Didn't Tell You*. New York: Context Books, 2003.

David Wurmser, *Tyranny's Ally: America's Failure to Defeat Saddam Hussein*. Washington, DC: AEI Press, 1999.

Periodicals

Ricardo Alonso-Zaldivar, "War with Iraq: In Harm's Way," *Los Angeles Times*, April 13, 2003.

Arms Control Today, "Iraq: A Chronology of UN Inspections and an Assessment of Their Accomplishments," October 2002.

Phyllis Bennis, "Half a Victory at the UN," *Nation*, December 2, 2002.

Joe Bleifuss, "Regime Change Begins at Home," *In These Times*, April 28, 2003.

John Cloud, "What's Fair in War?" *Time*, April 7, 2003.

Alan W. Dowd, "In Search of Monsters to Destroy: The Causes and Costs of the Bush Doctrine," *World & I*, January 2003.

Bobby Eberle, "Celebs Speak Their Mind and Expect Others to Keep Quiet," *Insight on the News*, May 13, 2003.

Economist, "The Hidden Menace: Iraq's Weapons," May 26, 2001.

———, "Rebuilding Iraq," April 19, 2003.

Reuel Marc Gerecht, "Why We Need a Democratic Iraq," *Weekly Standard*, March 24, 2003.

Paul Johnson, "French Kiss-Off," *National Review*, February 24, 2003.

Bill Keller, "Rumsfeld and the Generals," *New York Times*, April 5, 2003.

Paul Krugman, "Paths of Glory," *New York Times*, May 16, 2003.

Peter Mansbridge, "People Just Like You," *Maclean's*, April 21, 2003.

Monthly Review, "U.S. Imperial Ambitions and Iraq," December 2002.

Laurie Mylroie, "Iraq and America's Terrorist Threat," *World & I*, December 2001.

Geov Parrish, "What's Next," *In These Times*, May 19, 2003.

Anna Quindlen, "The Sounds of Silence," *Newsweek*, April 21, 2003.

Scott Ritter, interviewed by William Rivers Pitt, "Inspections: The Record," *Nation*, October 21, 2002.

William Shawcross, "Hard Jobs Require U.S. Power," *Los Angeles Times*, April 20, 2003.

Kenneth R. Timmerman, "What's Wrong with France?" *Insight on the News*, March 18, 2003.

Milton Viorst, "Why They Don't Want Democracy," *Los Angeles Times*, May 25, 2003.

Fareed Zakaria, "How to Wage War," *Newsweek*, April 21, 2003.

Index